ANIMATOR

By Jessica Cohn

Content Adviser: Jay Shultz, Layout Artist, Nickelodeon

Gareth Stevens
Publishing

Please visit our web site at **www.garethstevens.com**.
For a free catalog describing Gareth Stevens Publishing's list of high-quality books, call 1-800-542-2595 (USA) or 1-800-387-3178 (Canada).
Gareth Stevens Publishing's fax: 1-877-542-2596

Library of Congress Cataloging-in-Publication Data
Cohn, Jessica.
   Animator / by Jessica Cohn.
      p. cm. — (Cool careers: cutting edge)
   Includes bibliographical references and index.
   ISBN-10: 1-4339-1953-2   ISBN-13: 978-1-4339-1953-4 (lib. bdg)
   ISBN-10: 1-4339-2152-9   ISBN-13: 978-1-4339-2152-0 (soft cover)
   1. Animation (Cinematography)—Vocational guidance—Juvenile
   literature. 2. Cinematography—Special effects. I. Title.
   TR897.5.C643   2010
   791.43'34—dc22   2009002006

This edition first published in 2010 by
Gareth Stevens Publishing
A Weekly Reader® Company
1 Reader's Digest Rd.
Pleasantville, NY 10570-7000 USA

Copyright © 2010 by Gareth Stevens, Inc.

Executive Managing Editor: Lisa M. Herrington
Senior Editor: Brian Fitzgerald
Senior Designer: Keith Plechaty
Produced by Editorial Directions, Inc.
Art Direction and Page Production: Paula Jo Smith Design

Picture credits: Cover, title page, Eben Ostby/Science Faction; p. 4 Broccoli Photography/Alamy; p. 7 Content Mine International/Alamy; p. 8 Associated Press; p. 10 Tony Freeman/PhotoEdit Inc.; p. 14 Louis Quail/Corbis; p. 15 Hulton Archive/Getty Images; p. 16 TWPhoto/Corbis; p. 18 Trish Gant/Getty Images; p. 19 Marmaduke St. John/Alamy; p. 21 Photos 12/Alamy; p. 22 Spencer Grant/PhotoEdit Inc.; p. 23 Cre8tive Studios/Alamy; p. 24 Associated Press; p. 27 Kim Kulish/Corbis

Printed in the United States of America

1 2 3 4 5 6 7 8 9 14 13 12 11 10 09

CONTENTS

Words in the glossary appear in **bold** type the first time they are used in the text.

CHAPTER 1
SPECIAL EFFECTS

The star of *Wall-E* is a beat-up robot named Wall-E. Earth has become a garbage dump. Wall-E's job is to clean it up. At night, he stays in a warehouse. He plays a movie on an old TV. On the screen, a woman and man sing lovingly. They turn to one another and hold hands.

Have you ever thought of being an animator? Animators brought Wall-E to life on the big screen.

Wall-E watches carefully. He joins his hands together, as if he were holding someone's hand. Even though Wall-E is a cartoon character, you can feel his loneliness. This is the magic of animation.

Digital Daring

Chris Chua was an animator for *Wall-E*. He told a reporter about the pride he felt in the finished product. "All the great scenes are when you turn off that volume, and you know exactly what is going on even without sounds coming from the characters' mouths," he said.

Animators are artists who work to make cartoons appear to be alive. Animation artists often work with computers. They learn **digital** arts, which is art created on computers. Their main job is drawing and making models of characters. Animators express ideas and feelings through their work. They often make people laugh!

Chua worked as a fix animator on *Wall-E*. He polished the scenes after they were animated. Hundreds of animators worked on the movie. The next time you watch an animated film, pay attention to the credits that run at the end. Look at all the different names and jobs listed. Animation is usually a team effort.

Where Do Animators Work?

Some animators work in studios that develop projects from start to finish. Many animators work at places that produce the final edit, or cut, of a film or TV show. Some animators work from home.

An animator may work on anything from electronic greeting cards to big films. Some animators work in advertising. Other animation artists work on computer and video games or other interactive projects.

Are you cut out for this line of work? You must have strong art and computer skills to succeed. You need to be creative!

Is This Career Right for Me?

Animation is a cool career. Here are some questions to consider:

- Do you work well under pressure?
- Do you enjoy working as part of a team?
- Do you pay attention to details?
- Are you good at drawing or making models?
- Would you like to make money by using your imagination?

If your answers are yes, animation may be a good fit for you.

In True Form

When the film company Pixar made the
2003 movie *Finding Nemo*, its animators
had a hard job. Nemo and his friends are
underwater creatures. The artists had to
make the characters move in a believable
way. To do their work, the animators studied
many sea animals. They went diving in
Hawaii and visited fish tanks. In the end,
the characters moved like sea creatures yet
showed feelings like people!

CHAPTER 2

ANIMATION AT WORK

No two projects are the same in the field of animation. **Special effects animation** for a Super Bowl ad is different from a weekly cartoon show. Even so, all projects start with an idea.

Let's say you have an idea for a TV show. It stars a skeleton that lives among people and doesn't realize it is any different from humans. You know you can make this show funny.

You share your idea with others. They add their thoughts. You come up with a story that works. Next, you make plans to produce it. You look for a way to pay for it. This stage is called **development**.

Taking Steps

After development is the **preproduction** stage. Now the team decides on a certain look for the project. How much should the TV show look like a cartoon? How real will the skeleton and other figures seem?

The team writes a **script** to tell the story of your skeleton in the world of the living. Then an artist turns

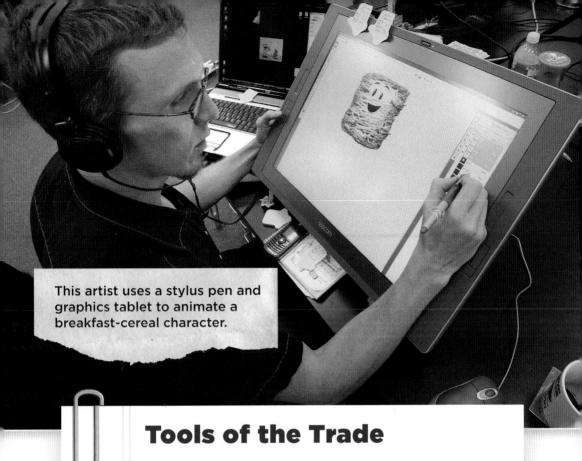

This artist uses a stylus pen and graphics tablet to animate a breakfast-cereal character.

Tools of the Trade

Animators use many different tools in their work. Many animators still sketch using pencil on paper. They also use a **stylus pen** on a **graphics tablet**. The stylus pen "draws" on the graphics tablet to change what's on the computer screen. Powerful computers help an animator draw without paper.

the script into a **storyboard**. This is a series of simple drawings that outline the basic story. It looks a lot like a comic strip.

A finished storyboard is just the start of the storyboard process. Animators do **animatics** to see what the story will look like on a screen. It is like taking a video of a storyboard. By running a camera over the images, animators can figure out how long the scenes take. They can also time the whole story of your skeleton's daily life.

Layout artists make drawings for each part of the story. These animators plan lighting, backgrounds, and camera angles.

On Board

No animation project goes forward without a storyboard that lays out the action. Animators make storyboards on large sheets of paper or on small cards. They pin the cards to a wall and move them around. Animators can create storyboards on a computer, too. One animated film can require thousands of storyboard drawings.

An animator reviews storyboards for a Charlie Brown cartoon.

Production and Postproduction

Production comes next. It involves another set of decisions. How will the skeleton move? What color should its eyes be? The team makes models of the characters to help them. They work carefully to give the characters personality.

Compositors take over during **postproduction**. They combine the different elements into single images. The compositors get things ready for the editors.

Editors finish the project. They make sure each change in scene flows into the next one. Sound editors add music and actors' voices to the images. Animation editors are artists who put the elements together. The skeleton you imagined has finally come to life on screen!

On a large team, each person has one role. On a small team, one animator often has many roles.

Working Together

Each step, from development to postproduction, has steps of its own. For example, animators often draw characters many different ways before settling on a final look. The team members do not always agree on creative decisions. Speaking up and sharing thoughts is part of a team member's job. The artists work together to come up with answers.

On the Job:
Animator Jay Shultz

Jay Shultz is a background design and layout artist at Nickelodeon, the cable TV network.

Q: How did you get into animation?

Shultz: It all started when I was seven years old. I saw *Star Wars*, and after that I just started drawing robots, spaceships, and aliens. I never stopped drawing from there. It was all I really wanted to do. I drew everything I could see or make up. Cartoons were my first step into art and my first love. It only seemed natural that I would have a career in animation.

Q: What do you do during a regular day?

Shultz: I draw the backgrounds and [settings] that the characters walk on in the show. Currently I'm working on *Dora the Explorer* and *Go, Diego, Go!*

Q: What do you most like about your job?

Shultz: I like researching and learning new things. I always find some new piece of information about a subject that I'm learning to draw.

Q: What is difficult about your career?

Shultz: The hardest thing to do is keep track of where everything hooks up with everything else. What that means is that making a cartoon is like building a car. We have many different parts of the cartoon being made at the same time. We put these parts together for the final products. You have to always be talking with the people on your crew to make sure that your scenes connect with theirs.

Q: What makes animation special?

Shultz: I actually make art that lives and moves. I get to create new and interesting worlds that people have never seen or could think of! I work in the type of job where you really don't have to grow up. In fact, the sillier you are, the better your cartoon will be.

Q: What would you tell students who are thinking about becoming animators?

Shultz: Draw as much as you can whenever you can. Don't stop drawing, even if you don't like what you are drawing. Just start over. Draw whatever you like or interests you. Draw the world around you, from people you know or see to buildings and forests that are around you — or in books. Learn how the natural world works by observing it. One of the best tools artists have is the ability ... to see the world and put it on paper.

CHAPTER 3

LIGHTS, CAMERA, ACTION!

Pictures in books and newspapers are 2-D, or two-dimensional. The images have height and width but appear flat. In the 1890s, people started putting flat images into movement on film. The first films were in black and white.

Soon after film was invented, moviemakers started playing with animated images. The first animation on standard film was in 1906. The short film's simple drawings showed two faces on a blackboard. The faces smiled and winked. Walt Disney came out with *Steamboat Willie*, the first cartoon with sound, in 1928.

Nick Park poses with clay models of Wallace and Gromit.

Ray Harryhausen works on stop-action animation in 1965.

Stop-Action

Ray Harryhausen started working in animation in the 1940s. He took photos of models making small moves. Each second of film captured 24 movements. This method is known as **stop-action**. Harryhausen is one of history's most important stop-action animators.

Many scenes in the first *Star Wars* movie used stop-action. A number of animators still work in this way. English animator Nick Park is one. Viewers love Park's films about Wallace, a cheese-loving inventor, and his dog Gromit.

Today, many popular TV programs, such as *The Simpsons*, are in 2-D animation. Animation comes in 3-D, too. The images have height, width, and depth. The *Shrek* films are examples of 3-D animation.

For Real

One of the biggest developments in animation was **computer-generated imagery (CGI)**. In 1995, Pixar's *Toy Story* became the first full-length movie made entirely with computer animation. Viewers were amazed. It was as if the animators had brought puppets to life.

These days, animators seem to be able to do almost anything using computers. Some animators create digital images so real they replace humans during dangerous action scenes. Some films, such as *The Polar Express* and *Beowulf*, feature famous actors whose characters are entirely animated.

Improvements in the Technology

Today's animators use greatly improved file formats. In the past, moving animation from one computer to another took a long time. Each frame added to the size of the file. Then came **graphic interchange format (GIF)**, which could do more with fewer images.

If you have ever seen a flip book, you know the basics of GIF animation. A flip book has a series of drawings that seem to move as the pages flip. GIF animation is similar but uses bold, simple images on a computer screen.

This animator uses computer-generated imagery (CGI). Her company produced the 2001 Japanese film *Spirited Away*.

A cartoon flip book makes 2-D images appear to move.

After GIF came the Flash format. Flash started as a way to create simple images that loaded quickly. Then Flash added even better features. It became a favorite with animators. Flash mixes images and sound. With Flash, animation sped up and stayed in high motion.

Using these tools and more, animators make worlds of their own in online games and on interactive sites. Now GIF and Flash are available to anyone with a computer. You can learn how to make animation, too. Using the Web, you can invite viewers into your own 3-D spaces.

A World of Your Own

To try stop-action animation, all you need is some basic equipment. You can use a digital video camera or digital still camera for stop-action. You need lights and something to set the camera on, such as a three-legged stand called a tripod.

Most of all, you need an idea and some puppets or models. Then you need software that lets you put the photos together. Nearly anything is possible with imagination — and plenty of time. Animators work years on some projects!

An animation class sets up clay figures. The students are using a digital camera on a tripod to shoot.

CHAPTER 4

GETTING INTO IT

The company PDI/DreamWorks spent almost three years producing the first *Shrek* movie. In *Shrek*, the team of animators brought a fairy tale to life. The animators wanted this fairy-tale world to look very real so viewers could relate to the characters.

Animator and producer Ken Bielenberg worked on the 2001 film. "For human characters, some of the challenges were [creating] skin," Bielenberg told an interviewer. The animators even made sure the animated clothing had wrinkles. All the little details added up to huge success.

Staging the Future

How do you get from where you are to where Bielenberg is? You don't have to wait to get started. You can draw characters and their different expressions and body poses. Most animation is rooted in the characters. So turn

Shrek animators used computers to model how fur, human hair, and grass move. It helped make the action look as real as possible.

A young artist draws at an animation table. Practice is the best way to improve your drawing skills.

on the storyteller within you. Make it a point to think up characters all the time.

You can make up a story or think of one people already know. Then make a storyboard about it. After you have drawn parts of the story, try filming the drawings. Or make cutouts from paper and film them. Remember that you are improving with each try.

It's important to take every opportunity to practice your skills. Learn about models and try to make them. Tabletop animation is making models and setting them on a tabletop for filming. Create sets for your models, too. Start with basic 2-D pictures of your models.

Animation for Medicine

Animation is part of many fields now. Rajeev Doshi studied medicine. Then a friend opened an animation school in New York, and Doshi took classes. The former medical student started animating things related to medicine.

His 3-D work appears in the book *Human Body*. "We love the fact that we can apply more modern visual [special effects] practices to the work we do and produce things that are more dynamic," he says.

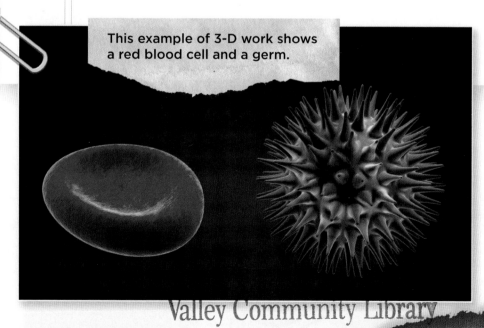

This example of 3-D work shows a red blood cell and a germ.

Tuned to Cartoons

Matt Groening created a comic strip that first appeared in a weekly Los Angeles newspaper in 1980. Soon the producer of a TV variety show asked the young artist to try animating for television. The Simpson family was born. Groening made his first animated Simpsons **short** for the show in 1987. Then Groening developed a half-hour TV show based on his shorts. *The Simpsons* celebrated 20 years on television in 2008.

Matt Groening arrives at the opening of *The Simpsons Movie* in 2007. He helped produce and write the film.

All Kinds of Opportunities

High school is your chance to sign up for more drawing, computer, film, or animation classes. At home, get comfortable operating a camera and telling stories on film. Join related clubs at your school. Search for student competitions, and give them your best shot. Look for summer camps that provide hands-on experience.

Career Cutout

Most successful animators have taken advanced classes in the arts. They have studied many subjects, including graphic design, electronic mixing, and digital sound. Technical schools offer animation courses. Some universities award bachelor's and graduate degrees in film and animation.

Most schools can steer you toward animation internships. Internships are unpaid jobs that offer valuable practical experience. You can learn from professional animators as well as show others how you work. Most major animation studios have some type of internship program.

To get an internship or a job, you will need to create a **demo reel**. A demo reel is clips of your best animation work to show employers.

CHAPTER 5

THE FINAL CUT

A nimation has become part of everyday life. That includes films, TV shows, video games, web sites, and advertising. Now people can become part of an animated life. How? They can visit a **virtual** world called Second Life.

Second Life characters are animated. They eat meals, go shopping, and drive cars online. The people who join the Second Life community decide how they want their characters to look and act. Things that happen in life as well as in imagination combine in this virtual world.

Virtual Classroom

The University of Southern California (USC) has a well-known film school with a degree in animation. Animation students take classes such as Introduction to 3-D Computer Animation. One class is called Designing Online Multiplayer Game Environments.

In 2008, USC animation students created a Second Life campus. The students set up a classroom and a screening room that are "open" to online visitors. The exercise helped prepare the students for careers. Much of the growth in animation will involve games and online communities, such as Second Life.

Putting It Together

Animation's possibilities seem endless. Someday soon, animation will probably change the way kids learn in school. Careers in animation will grow in ways we can only imagine. Using animation, young thinkers are finding countless ways to mix life with art.

Technically Ready

Animators study life to make art. They study technology to bring their art to life. An animator can draw a character in a pose. Then the animator can let a computer draw movements before and after that pose.

A computer can make "bones" for the creatures an animator draws. The bones look

Did you know there are animation classes online? Many college-age people learn animation from experts on the Web.

like frames of wire on the screen. Animators can give those bones movement. The artists can use the bones to help move the images of their creatures. That way, the images look more real.

To become an animator, you need to learn how to use all the tools of animation. An animation career combines storytelling, practical skills, and the latest technology.

New Worlds

If you are interested in this career, search the Internet to find out more about animation schools. You do not have to wait until your college years to "animate" your future, however. Get a book. Get a video-based teaching course. Tell your stories in images of your own making.

On the Go!

Video game animators are at the cutting edge of the business. The latest challenge for these animators is mobile gaming, including games on cell phones. Animating the next best thing will take new kinds of thinking.

Career Fact File

ANIMATOR

OUTLOOK

- The job outlook is good for animators with digital and computer skills. In 2006, about 87,000 multimedia artists and animators were working in the United States. By 2016, there will be about 110,000.

- About 10 percent of U.S. film industry workers are self-employed. Many small companies use contractors. So you may find yourself working from contract to contract.

WHAT YOU'LL DO

- Animators need imagination and hands-on skills. They bring stories to life. They learn everything they can about special effects and computers. Then they apply their skills to a wide range of film, TV, and Web projects.

- Animators design images for broadcast and the Web. They design games and CD-ROMs. Some animators have jobs in TV and film, working on characters, effects, and backgrounds. A few animators even help create amusement rides!

WHAT YOU'LL NEED

- Take classes in graphic design. Make sure to study digital sound, electronic mixing, and animation. Formal training programs in technical schools and universities are best. A bachelor's or graduate degree can help open doors.

WHAT YOU'LL EARN

- In 2007, most animators and multimedia artists earned more than $54,000. The highest 10 percent earned more than $98,000. This does not include the salaries of those who work for themselves.

Sources: U.S. Department of Labor, Bureau of Labor Statistics; *Princeton Review*

GLOSSARY

animatics — storyboards shown in motion on tape or film to determine timing

compositors — workers who combine the different elements into single images for a film or TV show

computer-generated imagery (CGI) — pictures produced by computer

demo reel — clips of an animator's best work

development — the first stage of production when an idea becomes a script with funding

digital — created on computers

graphic interchange format (GIF) — a computer file format that stores simple, bold images best

graphics tablet — a flat screen that an animator "draws" on with a stylus pen to enter images and graphics into a computer

layout artists — animators who design the backgrounds, lighting, and camera angles of a film or TV show

postproduction — the stage of production that ends in the final cut

preproduction — the stage of production when hiring, finalizing the script, and scheduling takes place

production — the process of producing a film or TV program

script — the written text of a cartoon or other piece of animation

short — a brief film

special effects animation — animation that produces a desired impression in a scene, such as an earthquake or a snowstorm

stop-action — animation in which film or video captures a model moving bit by bit

storyboard — a series of simple drawings that outline a basic story

stylus pen — a pointed instrument that animators use to "draw" on a graphics tablet

virtual — created by means of a computer

TO FIND OUT MORE

Books

Marcovitz, Hal. *Computer Animation.* Detroit: Lucent Books, 2008.

Parks, Peggy. *Computer Animator.* Detroit: KidHaven Press, 2006.

Rauf, Don, and Monique Vescia. *Virtual Apprentice! Cartoon Animator.* New York: Ferguson, 2007.

Thompson, Lisa. *Art in Action: Have You Got What It Takes to Be an Animator?* Minneapolis: Compass Point Books, 2008.

Web Sites

Amazing Kids! Animation Station

www.amazing-kids.org/anicon00_12-14.htm

Watch animations created by kids and teens.

Animation Mentor

www.animationmentor.com

Look for free resources for all levels of animators.

FluxTime Studio: Animations

www.fluxtime.com

Check out these free animation activities. Create your own animation.

National Gallery of Art Kids: Flip Book

www.nga.gov/kids/stella/activityflip.htm

Learn how to make your own flip book.

INDEX

About the Author

Jessica Cohn lives in Westchester County, New York, where she runs a publishing firm. The work allows her to research interesting topics and think about new ideas, which is one of her favorite things in life. She has written books about many kinds of jobs, from aerospace workers to vocational teachers. Every job is interesting, she says, when you look at it closely!